Our Love Is...

The C. R. Gibson Company
Norwalk, Connecticut

Our love is...

How shall I start? Our love is too big for any simple, easy definition or explanation. Sometimes I feel as if our love is "another person." "Someone you and I have created by meeting, by being drawn to each other and, finally, by loving." This "other person," our love, is part of me and part of you. But somehow this being that

has come out of us is greater than both of us put together. Sometimes we lead and direct our love. And at other times our love leads us. Easily and naturally, we follow.

Our love has part of my personality, part of yours and another part that is all its own.

Our love can be happy and carefree at one moment, serious and thoughtful in the next. It can be comforting to both of us, reassuring. Then at other times it can be a little

Frightening, speeding us
along a little faster than we
may choose on the way to
closeness and intimacy.
Our love is braver than either
one of us alone might be.
Willing to take risks that
neither of us would have been
willing to venture before.
Love makes us both open up,
admit our weaknesses, reach
out to each other with complete
honesty and trust.
Our love can be on the silly
side, too, laughing, making
us both laugh along.

It definitely has a mind of
its own. And many times
our love isn't reasonable
or careful. It's unpredictable
and even kind of scary —
more fun than anything
else in the world

To describe it, all of it, would be
almost impossible. It's just
too varied, too changeable, too
complex.

But here are a few thoughts
about this wonderful, many-
sided feeling we share. Put
together, perhaps they can
paint a portrait of our love.

Our Love Is...A Beautiful Thing

When I think of beautiful
things, I think of things
I can see — a flower,
multi-colored sunset,
wildflowers, butterflies —
things I can hear — a
favorite piece of music, the
tide coming in, children
laughing — things I can
touch — the soft richness
of velvet, the furrowed
veins of old wood

All these beautiful things are made known by the senses. But not our love. And it is more beautiful than any-thing else in the world

Love goes deeper than the senses. We can't see it or hear it or touch it. Its beauty is made known to us by a sixth sense that exists only in the heart. Trying to describe the beauty of love to anyone who hasn't experienced it just can't be done.

If would be like trying to describe an exotic fruit to someone

who had never tasted it.
I could tell about its size
and shape, talk about its
color and texture. But the
essence of the fruit would
be beyond explaining. Just
as the essence, the real beauty
of love can be known only
to those who truly experience it.
The beauty of love reaches out
to affect every area of life.
Now, thanks to you and
love, all the things I used
to admire are made more
vivid, more beautiful than
ever before.

I can listen to some of my old
favorite records and hear
music that I never knew
was there.

Colors are brighter and bolder.
Before you, the world was
pale, like a water color. Now
it is deeply and strikingly
colorful, with the richness
of an oil painting.

Our love is a beautiful thing,
known only to the depth
sense of the heart, but it
has renewed all my other
senses to the beauty that
has always been around me.

Because of you, now I don't
merely listen — I hear.
Instead of just looking,
I see. Instead of only
touching, I feel.
Because of you, because of
the beauty of our love.

Our Love Is A Happy, Funny Thing

Has anyone ever told you that
you're a pretty funny person?
Well, you are. (And I don't
mean funny-strange.)

There are a lot of things
about you that make me
smile and laugh and feel
happy every time I'm near
you.
You have funny ways of
saying things that are
just different enough from
the way everyone else talks
to get me kind of tickled.
I like it!
And you get funny expressions
on your face when you're
surprised or puzzled or
when you're concentrating
very hard.

Sometimes, when I'm not with you, I'll start thinking about some of those funny things you do and I'll start laughing right out loud. But don't get me wrong. Those funny things you say and do that make you you are parts of you I love best of all.

You must think I'm pretty funny, too, in some ways. I know there are times when I'm talking to you and I'll see you thinking for no reason at all. Maybe

you are even start laughing
And I don't mind a bit
Because we both do things
that are pretty amusing.
And we do them without
even knowing it. It's just
part of our personalities.
And that makes our love
a happy, funny thing.
Love is pretty serious a lot of
the time — but not all the
time. If it was I think it
might be kind of a strain
after a while. But we don't
ever have to worry about that
Some of our best times are the

laughter times, the playful,
silly times.

As we put together our book
of memories, the part about
laughter will probably be
one of our favorites — right
now I can think of so many
happy times we've spent
together just laughing,
having fun, being child-
like (not childish) with
each other.

I can remember times when
we've spent hours just
people-watching. It's so
much fun with you, at

someplace where there are
lots of people passing,
like a shopping center. We
can watch people go by and
talk about the funny things
about them — not in a
mean way — just noticing
all the different ways that
people can be funny.
I remember so many funny
things we've done on the
spur of the moment.
Maybe you'd say — "Let's
go to the drive-in and see
the triple horror movie
spectacular!" And I'll

say, "OK!" and we're on our way.

I remember all the silly jokes we've played on each other, the gag gifts we've given each other.

And I remember all our private jokes, the things that are funny just to you and me. If something reminds us of one of them, no one else can ever figure out what we're laughing at. Somebody said that there is the most fun you can have without laughing. Well,

My Love, My Friend

It may sound strange to say
this, but there are probably
many people who love each
other (sort of) even though
they don't like each other
very much at all.
I say love each other (sort of)
because that kind of love

we've got love and laughter—
that's the most fun of all.
And that's no joke!

is a kind of flimsy, synthetic version of the real thing.

In order to really love some-one, you've got to like that person too. You're got to have that winning combina-tion of love ... and friendship. Like we do!

You're not only the one I love. You're my best friend too. I really like you. And if I didn't, I could never love you the way I do, with all of my heart.

If we only loved each other, it

we weren't such good friends,
our relationship would be
only a part of what it
should be, of what it is.
Love without friendship grows
old pretty fast. Imagine
day after day of watching
but romance. Every meal
a candlelight occasion,
with wine and music.
Every conversation a "love"
conversation. Always
looking into each other's
eyes, but never looking
outward, together, in the
same direction.

Love without friendship is
being always dressed up,
always feeling your best.
It's feeling awkward a lot
because so often you run
out of anything to say.
It's very serious, very intense,
uneasy much of the time,
and, quite often, boring.
But best of us — in love with
each other and best friends,
too. We can be romantic
some times (and I like
that a lot) and when we feel
like it, we can just take it
easy and have fun.

We have so many things to
talk about besides each
other I can't imagine an
awkward silence with you
We never have enough
time to talk about all the
things we want to.
Because we're friends, there
are so many things for
us to share, so many
things to laugh about
And I always feel so relaxed
and easy with you. I like
it when I'm reading my
best but I like the other
times, too. Say if we decide

to wash the car and we
both have on old jeans and
we get wet and dirty and
feel really giddy. Friends
like to be that way with
each other. Friends who love
each other like to be any
old way in the world, as
long as they're together.
I love having you but I'm so
glad I like you, too. And
that you like me. Why,
even if I didn't love you,
I'd still want to be your
friend.
But this way is best of all.

Our Love Is A Secret Thing

In other times, when I've thought
I was in love, the first thing
I wanted to do was talk
about it. I wanted to confide
in my friends, share with

You're my love, my friend
And because of that, ours
is the best kind of love,
whole and complete. One
that I truly believe will
last for a long, long time.

them the feelings that I thought I was feeling. Probably, I wanted to broad-cast my fervor because I was so proud to be experiencing the mysterious emotions that I had known before only second hand, from movies and books and stories in magazines.

"Hey," — Maybe I wanted to say, — "Hey, look at me. I'm all grown up now. I can love!"

And when you tell someone about something you're not really so sure of, it seems to

make it more real—at least during the feeling.

But the more I talked about the way I was feeling, the more I began to doubt that I was really in love at all.

It was like slowly letting the air out of a beautiful but very insubstantial balloon.

Now I feel differently. In so many ways, our love is a secret thing to me, a thing that belongs to nobody else but us.

That's not to say that I don't talk about you. I do. There's

no way, I could help but tell
my friends about you because
you make me so very proud.
But even though I talk quite
a bit about you, in glowing
terms, I don't say very
much at all about us.
There are things you've said
to me or written me in a
letter that I've never repeated
to anyone. So many of the
days and evenings we're
shared, so many of our
plans and dreams are
secrets that I don't want
to share with others. They

belong to us and spreading them around would seem like bragging and would cheapen them somehow. Also, I've found out something about happiness — real happiness. When you finally experience it, it's just kind of pointless to talk about it. It would be like going out on a very clear sunny day and telling your friends — "Look. The sun is shining." Now, so often, people tell me "You look so happy," or

"You sounded so happy
over the phone yesterday.
It must be love."
Well, it is. But I don't tell
anyone about it. Just a look
at my face and they know
that very well. The way I
feel about you is a secret
I can't keep but share.
But all the rest of our world
is very private and personal
to me. There are things that
we have known together
that are just too precious
to ever tell anyone else. Our
love is a secret thing and

Our Love Is A Mysterious Thing

There are mysteries about
our love, things that
neither one of us may ever
understand because love
is an emotion that is
beyond understanding.
We know we love each other
but we could never explain,

our words, our hopes, our
dreams, our joys ... are for
you and me alone.

completely, why we love each other.

Love isn't like a clock. You can't take it apart to see what makes it tick. And if you could, preferably you could never get it back together again.

There's no barometer to measure love, no thermometer, no scale, no standard, no rule. There's no litmus test for love. No one can ever chart the course of love. But when love finds two people worthy, then it will direct their course.

What else in the world, besides love, could make two people who, in order that they both become two people? Mathe-matically, that just doesn't make sense. But then love doesn't make much sense. On the other hand, it is the only thing that makes any sense at all.

People who say that love is kind must have been kind to love. Love does more, not less. And because it does more, it is capable of accepting a whole person

and not just a few outstand-
ing qualities.

Love can never be described to someone who hasn't experi-enced it. You have to be there. And if you haven't been there, you may want to like those who say — "There is much talk of love and ghosts by people who have never seen either one."

I've never seen a ghost but I've been "love." I know it's real. I'm not sure how I know but I'm more sure of love than I am of many things

I can see or hear or touch.
Still, love is a mystery to me
in many respects. One that
I will never completely
understand.
But one thing I do know —— I
am very glad to be sharing
this mysterious feeling with
someone as wonderful as you.

How Do I Know I Love You?

When did I first know that I
loved you? That's hard for

me to say. Bits and pieces
of my feelings for you came
together a little at a time
until suddenly the whole
picture was clear to me.
Then I knew I loved you.
But how did I know?
How do I know now?
I know I love you because I feel
a new kind of poetry within
me. You I feel as if I could
write a poem that is full of
meaning and beauty. But I
really don't need to because,
in a wonderful way, the two of
us are already a poem.

I know I love you because now
it doesn't really matter to
me where we are or what we
are doing — as long as
we're together...

...because every time we meet
it is like a celebration and all
the things we do are fun.
I know I love you because I don't
feel the need to prove anything
anymore...

...because I never want to
change you. I only want you
to be the real you, me to be the
real me, so we can be the
real us.

I know I love you because all
my old loves for family and
friends are stronger now.
And because my heart is
open to love just about every-
one and everything in the
world. Just as everyone seems
to love a lover, a lover just
naturally loves everyone back.
I know I love you because I
never sit around deliberating
about whether this is the
real thing or not...
...because I never have to rely on
pulling daisy petals or twist-
ing straws to check on how

you feel about me. Just being
with you tells me all I need
to know.

I know I love you for a hundred
reasons and then some too
many to tell you all of them
now. I'll save the others
for other times.

But just one more. This one is
the simplest and the best.
I know I love you because
now in a place where there
was no feeling at all
before, in the deepest part
of my heart... I know
I know.

Our Time is Now

The long past, that that time before
we knew each other is like
atom now. There is no
changing a minute of it.
The future is unseen, hidden
around the next bend of
our lives. There's no way
to prophesy what it may
hold.

But now is real. It is here.
It is happening. And we
should live every second
of it. Fare every minute of it
Then when it slips into the

world of yesterday, it will hold only good memories and never "might-have-been's."

Saying that we should live and love in the _now_ doesn't mean that we shouldn't turn back occasionally and see where we've been. That's the only way we can keep from making the same mistakes twice.

And we need to plan, to dream. But we should never get so absorbed in what lies ahead that we neglect the beauty

of the present moment
This reminds that we're
sharing is more precious
than any part of gold that
might be at the end of it
Right now you are reading
these words that tell you
some of the ways I feel
Maybe I'm beside you. If
not, my thoughts are near.
And this very moment is
unique and beautiful.
Our time is now. It doesn't
matter as much what
we're doing as long as we're
doing it together.

If we're talking or walking,
seeing friends or dreaming
alone together, I want us to
bring the present moment
and never loosen its meaning
with too many thoughts of
other times, other faces,
other voices, other reams.
Some people are so cautious
with their fare. They measure
it out, little by little.
Thinking that when it is gone
there won't be any more.
But fare isn't like that. I can
give you all mine now (and
I do) — you can give me all

yours — and we'll both
have more than we started
with.

How wonderful to have a
treasure that always
replenishes itself.

How great to live in the split-
second clarity of the present
moment, to really live life,
not edited like some TV
movie, but _live_, while it
happens.

How happy I am to know that
right this very minute —
we are — love is! Our time
is now!

written by
Dean Walley

photographed by
Marianna Nolan

Photo Credits

Maria Demarest—Cover, p. 26; Michael Powers—p. 2, p. 55; Four By Five, Inc.—p. 6, p. 23, p. 31, p. 42, p. 51; Elizabeth P. Welsh—p. 11; Stanford Burns—p. 15; Don Davenport—p. 19; Jay Johnson—p. 35; Klaus Brahmst—p. 38.